SONATA in G

For Oboe and Piano

Figured bass realized by
A. GIBILARO

I

G. SAMMARTINI
Edited and arranged by
EVELYN ROTHWELL

II

Allegro assai

SONATA in G

For Oboe and Piano

Figured bass realized by
A. GIBILARO

I

G. SAMMARTINI
Edited and arranged by
EVELYN ROTHWELL

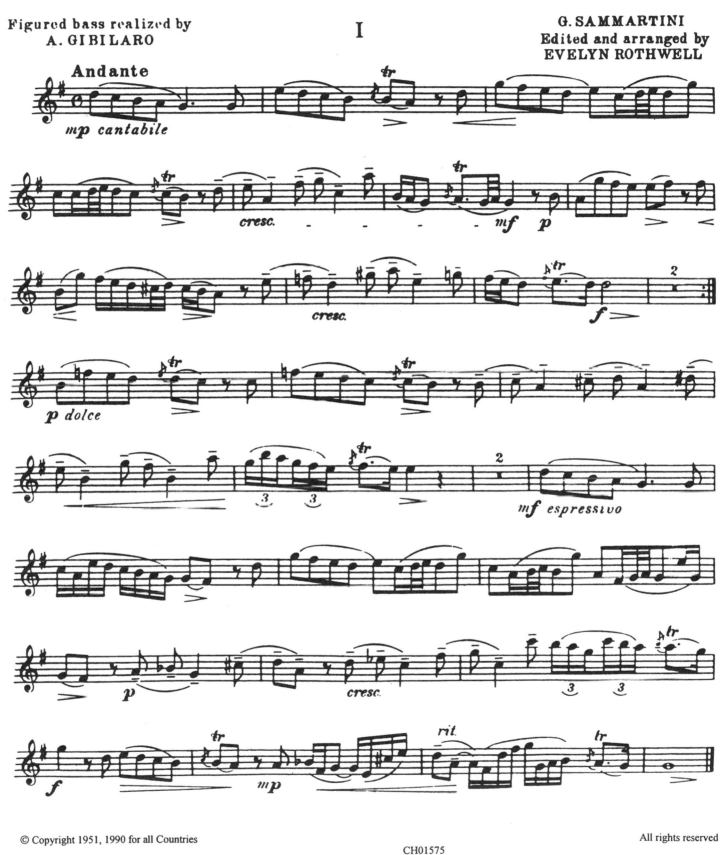

CH01575

II

Allegro assai

III

IV

Andante Lento

mp cantabile

mp cantabile

cresc.

p espress.

mp espressivo

espressivo

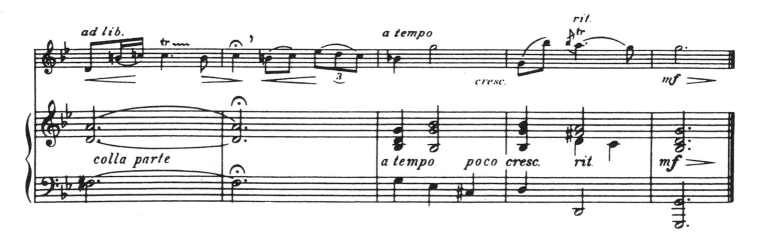

IV

Allegro